TO LISTEN IS TO HEAL

Albert J. Nimeth O.F.M

FRANCISCAN HERALD PRESS

1434 WEST 51st STREET • CHICAGO, 60609

TO LISTEN IS TO HEAL by Albert J. Nimeth O.F.M. Copyright ©1984 by Franciscan Herald Press, 1434 W. 51st Street, Chicago, Illinois 60609. Made in the United States of America. All rights reserved.

Library of Congress Number:

BV647.L56N55   1984   28.4   83-20669
ISBN 0-8199-0874-6

Nihil Obstat:
Mark Hegener O.F.M.
Censor Librorum

Imprimi potest:
Dismas Bonner O.F.M.
Minister Provincial

PUBLISHED WITH ECCLESIASTICAL PERMISSION

2 3 4 5 6 7 8 9 REPRINTS

TO LISTEN IS TO HEAL

Dedication:

To John Scott S.J. *of the Creighton Community whose personal interest and enthusiastic support came at a time when most needed.*

Gratitude:

To Kay Kueltzo *for the line drawings and artwork.*

To Carol Kroll *for patient typing and retyping of the manuscript.*

To Lydia Mack *for meaningful and fruitful discussions.*

TABLE OF CONTENTS

1. *Silence* 11
2. *God* 17
3. *Love* 23
4. *Self* 31
5. *Our Body* 40
6. *Potential* 47
7. *Habits* 53
8. *Nature* 57
9. *Forgiveness* 65
10. *Joy* 71
11. *Compliments* 77
12. *Humor* 82
13. *Music* 87
14. *Teenagers* 95
15. *Divorced* 102
16. *Elderly* 107
17. *Bereaved* 114

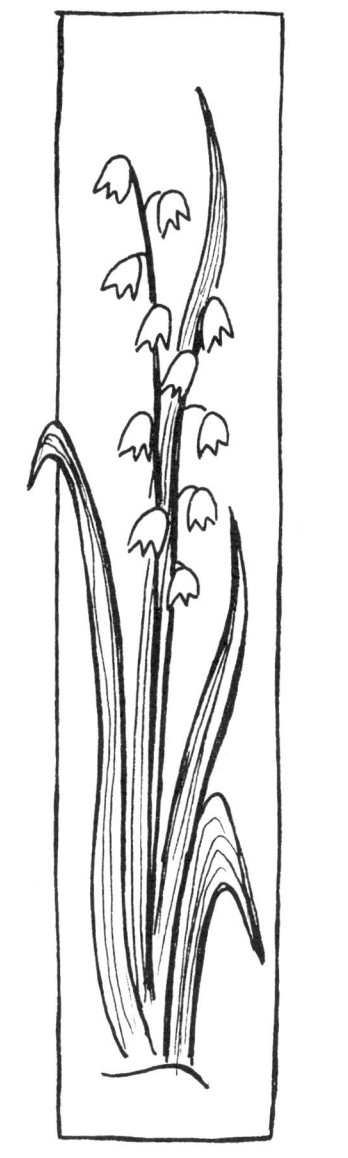

PART I

TO LISTEN IS TO HEAL.
We can heal ourselves
    if we learn to listen
        with our ears
        with our eyes
        with our minds
        with our feelings
        with our love.

It is important
    that we listen
        to God's love in our heart,
        to God's voice in our conscience.

It is healing
    to listen
        to our self-value,
        to our bodies,
        to our habits,
        to our potential.

This discovery
> will help us
>> heal ourselves.

Silence helps us
> get next to ourselves,
> live more than
>> surface existence.

The rapidity of communication,
> the instant newsbreak,
> tomorrow's news — tonight,
>> tend to make us
>> live on the periphery,
>>> on the surface.

Too many of us
> are like a barometer;
> we register change
>> but do not influence it.

Only in silence
> can we go
> deeper
>> to recoup waning strength,
>> to sharpen awareness,
>> to live more meaningfully.

When we make a phone call,
> we try to shut out the noise,
>> so we can converse
>>> intelligently,
>>> without interruption.

What therapy
> we can find
>> in the symphony of nature,
>> in the music that surrounds us,
>> in the humor of living.

We have to listen
> in silence,
> in prayer,
> at work,
> in the noise.

To listen
> is to heal.

1 – SILENCE

WE CAN HELP
    heal ourselves
        by listening
            to silence.

From time to time
    we have to turn off
        the agitated stirring
        of the hectic world.
We have to allow ourselves
    to rest
        in silence.
It is necessary
    to retire
        to our private desert place.

Our world is
    talkative,
    garrulous.
Everywhere the noise
    and excitement
        distract us
        from ourselves.

We even welcome
    the noise
        to avoid meeting ourselves.

We cannot
    forever
        run away from ourselves.
If we do,
    we will never
        truly live with reality.
To meet ourselves
    we need
        silence,
        peace,
        quiet.

If we cannot
    get extended periods,
        we snatch at the short ones.

We do not always
    have to be talking
    to enjoy life.

A mirror never speaks,
    but it grasps
        the glory of a sunset,
        the delicacy of a flower,
        the interest of a face.
In silence
    we can discover
    these wonders
        and more wonders about ourselves.

Only if we shut out
    distraction,
    interruption,
        can we commune
            with ourselves,
            with our God,
            with the wonders around us.

Great things
    happen
        in silence.
In silence
    Mary responded to her call.
    God entered human history.
In silence
    a sinner realizes
        a need for redemption.
In silence
    we find and accept
             love.
In silence
    this love can grow.

To hear ourselves
    we have to tread
        softly.

Self speaks
>   in the gentle whisper
>   of a zephyr.

To hear ourselves
>   is necessary.

Even though
>   fraught with anxiety,
>   it is in listening to ourselves
>   >   that we meet reality.

It is important
>   that we live
>   with reality.

In silence,
>   we meet ourselves.

This is good.
This is healing.

2 – GOD

WE CAN HEAL OURSELVES
    if we listen
        to God.

So much of our distress arises
    because
        we have lost touch
            with God.
We need
    the sure and reliable guidance
    that comes
        from the voice
        of God.

Because so much of life is
    in flux and flow,
        we need firm anchors
        on which to base our lives.
We need firm pegs
    around which
    our lives can revolve
        and which
        give a sense of direction.

We need
    an absolute
        to give us stability.
This is God.

We have to listen
    to God
        as we encounter him
        in our prayer life.

Most of us,
    in prayer,
        voice our needs,
            our hopes,
            our wants,
            our fears,
            our desires.
We express
    our sorrow,
    our thanksgiving.

This is
    the talking side
        of prayer.
There is also
    a listening side.

If we listen
    we will hear
    God's response
        in the form of inspiration,
            of insight,
            of perception,
            of perspective.

We can listen to God
    in Sacred Scripture,
    in the voice of his church.

We can listen to God
    in the secret recesses
        of our souls
        where our conscience
            registers approval,
                disapproval.

This it does
    according to the value system
    that directs
        our sense of right,
            of wrong.

If we listen to our conscience,
    which echoes
        the voice of God,
        we can heal many hurts
            emotional,
            psychological,
            spiritual.

All the more reason
    why
    we must form
        a correct conscience
        in the light of religious consensus,
            of accumulated experience
                of men of good will.

A correct conscience is *not*
    too strict, rigid, scrupulous,
    too loose, lenient, lax.
Understand the principles
    and apply them
        with discretion,
        with common sense.

If silence evades us,
    let's look for God
        in the noise,
        in the turmoil,
        in the feverish activity.
God can be found
    anywhere.
Listen to him
    wherever
        we find him.
In finding God
    we find the ultimate source
        of peace,
        of happiness,
        of healing.

3 – LOVE

GOD OWES MAN NOTHING
He is totally superior to
    and completely independent
        of man.
Man adds
    nothing
        to God's glory
        any more than a candle
        adds to the brilliance of the sun.

Then why are we here?

God was
    under no compulsion
    to create us.

In seeking an answer
    we run smack up against
        the most mystifying,
        the most amazing,
        the most puzzling
            enigma of God's love.

God is love!

Love, by its nature, is
    diffusive,
    expansive,
    brimming up,
    spilling over.

We are here because
    of the extravagance,
    of the prodigality
        of God's love.

So much does God love
    that he made
    you and me
        after his own image.
He wanted
    more of himself
        to love.
You and I
    are not loved
        as a glob of humanity.
You and I
    are loved individually,
    as if there was
        no one else to love.

Of all the countless,
    possible human beings
    God could have created,
        but did not,
            he created you and me.

Of you and me he said:
    "There is someone I love"
    "There is someone I want."
        "I love you and want you
        not only for a time
            but for eternity."

In the very act of creating us
    God implants
        the seeds of immortality.
In his love for us
    God endows us
        with marvelous equipment
            of body,
            of soul,
            of mind,
            of spirit.

In Hamlet we read:
    "What a piece of work is man. How noble in reason! How infinite in faculty! In form and moving how express and admirable. In action how like an angel! In apprehension how like a god! The beauty of the world! The paragon of animals."

In a burst of generosity
    God snatches us up
        to his very bosom,
            raises us up to his level,
            gives us a spark
            of his divine life.

Even if
    we desert him
        God does not abandon us.
Through the magnificent gesture
    of Calvary
        he restores us
           to life,
           to love.

Once again
    he gives us the opportunity
        to be with him forever,
           to attain ultimate fulfillment.

Through his prophet he assures us:
    "I have loved you with an everlasting love therefore I have drawn you to myself, taking pity upon you."

He never gives up.

"Love wist to pursue, still with unhurrying chase; and unperturbed pace, deliberate speed, majestic instancy, came those following feet."

                — Francis Thompson

If God has so loved us,
    we must be lovable.
If God has accepted us,
    we must be acceptable.

We do well
>   to appreciate our worth,
>   to acknowledge our value,
>   to love ourselves.

Self-love is
>   necessary,
>   legitimate,
>   wholesome.

"Love your neighbor
>   as
>   you love yourself."

We love ourselves
>   by taking care of our needs —
>   our physical needs,
>   but if we stop there,
>   we become selfish;
>   our emotional needs,
>   but if we stop there,
>   we become narcissistic;
>   our intellectual needs,
>   but if we stop there,
>   we become egotistical.

We must include
>   our spiritual needs.

These sanctify all other needs.
We have to consider
>   the total person
>   and not fragmentize.

Many of us are in trouble
    emotionally,
    psychologically,
    spiritually
        because
            we do not love ourselves
                    enough!

If we learn
    to love ourselves,
        as we should,
            we will listen to
                all the love around us.
We will be open
    and accepting
        when others assure us
        that they love us.
We need this love.
We need to know we are loved.

If we accept God's love,
    if we accept we are loveable,
        we have the basis
        for accepting love from others.

It is healthy
    and healing
        to listen to this love.

4 – SELF

LISTENING TO OURSELVES
    is a way
    to help heal ourselves.

To achieve peace of mind,
    to gain a measure of contentment,
    we have to listen to the answers
        we give to these questions:
            Who am I?
            What am I?
            Why am I?
            Where am I going?
            How do I get there?

If we listen
    to our answers,
    we get a deeper understanding
        of our uniqueness.

Each of us
    has a fund of gifts.
Each of us
    has special talents.
Each of us
    has individual opportunities.

To underestimate
    our true worth
    creates hurt.
To heal the hurt,
    we have to accept
        our real worth.

To be sure
    we all have
    our hangups and foibles.
These often
    are confused and confusing.
We have to learn
    to distinguish
        between the real and imaginary.
If we listen
    carefully
        we will stop beating the air;
        we will stop wasting time
            in pointless struggle.

If we listen to ourselves,
    we keep in touch
        with past memories of successes.
These memories
    beget
    confidence
        for the present and future.

The challenge is
    to really listen.

We are saturated with cacophony
    that intrudes
        upon the quiet
            of our soul
We are uncomfortable
    with silence.
We keep our radios blaring
    in varying decibels
        at home,
        away from home,
        at all points in between.
If we cannot capture
    moments of silence,
        let's listen to ourselves
        in the noise.

What we hear
    may come as a surprise,
        much like the first time
        we hear our recorded voice.
We don't believe
    what we hear.

To heal ourselves
    we have to believe
    what we hear —
        the miscues and mistakes
        because these are part of reality.

But we must also hear
>   the good,
>   the gifts,
>   the love,
>   the acceptance.
These too
>   are part of reality.

We have to listen to
>   our emotions and feelings.
They are an essential part
>   of human existence.
Without our emotions and feelings
>   life would be
>   dull,
>   monotonous.

These give life
>   nuances,
>   point,
>   counterpoint.
Because of emotions and feelings
>   no two moments
>   ever are the same.

It is a pity
>   to attempt
>   to eliminate
>   emotions and feelings.

I AM UNIQUE, LORD

I am unique, Lord, for I am the expression of your love, and no two moments of love are ever the same. Each is separate, intimately personal. Each is an original inimitable reflection of your own love-laden personality.

And because I am unique, Lord, I have a unique contribution to make to your love-mission on earth.

There are people whom only I can love in the way that counts — people waiting for my touch, eyes searching for my look of understanding, hands reaching for my extended strength, arms waiting for my embrace.

Lord, what mystery and magnificence! That you should take my unique weakness and use it as a means of communicating your unique power, that you should select one who needs to be saved and use him to save others.

Lord, I am so utterly proud of my individual treasure. My divinely lonely talents, to be that mirrored glance of you which alone can save a sinner.

Empower me, Lord. Cast out shadows so that only beauty and brightness go forth from the unique me to another you.

A stoic stance
    that finds
    feeling and emotions
        intolerable
        in self or others
            is unnatural,
            inhuman,
            destructive.
It is healthy
    and human
        to acknowledge,
        to accept
            our emotions and feelings.

Because we are
    rational beings
        we learn to live
        with our emotions and feelings.

Our task
    concerning emotions and feelings
        is not to crush, but control;
        not to repress, but to regulate;
        not to strangle, but to subject.

We have to accept ourselves
    as we are.
We may be
    different from others,
    but that does not make us
        less worthy.

No two snowflakes
    are alike
        yet each is beautiful.
No two sunsets
    are alike
        yet each is glorious.
No two human beings
    are alike
        yet each has a glory;
        each has a beauty
            we must accept
                and appreciate.

When we listen
    to ourselves
        carefully,
        honestly,
            we discover
            our glory,
            our beauty.

It is healing
    to listen
        to ourselves.

5 – OUR BODY

TO HEAL OURSELVES
> we have to
>> listen
>> to our body.

We are God's masterpiece,
> created a little
>> less than the angels.

It is necessary
> that we keep in touch
> with our needs
>> and provide for them.

This is self-love.
We love ourselves
> by taking care of ourselves.
The most obvious needs
> are our physical needs.

If we listen
> to our body,
> we discover
>> we need rest.
Everybody ought to learn
> to rest and relax.

Relaxing is not doing something;
    it is allowing something
        to happen to you.
It is passive
    not active.
It is letting muscles unwind
    and go limp and loose.
Easy does it! **
We cannot drive
    our body
        relentlessly
        without disaster.

Doctor says:
    "You are burning your candle
        at both ends."
Instead of adjusting
    we ask for
        a bigger candle.

Our body
    is not immortal.
It wears down.
It wears out.

We need time
    to recoup spent energy,
    to regain strength,
    to replenish healing powers.

**See page 123

For this
>   we need rest.
We have to listen
>   when our body
>   demands rest.
We also need
>   proper diet.
Too many are overfed
>   and undernourished.

Proper eating habits
>   demand
>   >   we provide
>   >   all necessary elements.

Proper eating
>   also means
>   >   we do not overeat.
The perpetual battle of the bulge
>   can be enervating.

"Hi diddle diddle
  I'm watching my middle
  hoping to whittle it soon,
  but eating is such fun
  twill never be done
  til the dish runs away
      with the spoon."

We all know
>   that a daily physical
>   exercise program
>   is needed.
For this we have to
>   overcome inertia,
>   overcome indolence.
This may be difficult.
This requires self-discipline.
If we listen
>   attentively
>   to our body needs,
>   we will pay this price
>   of self-discipline
>   because it will pay off.

We certainly
>   are not listening to our body
>   when we ingest drugs.
As a people,
>   we take more drugs
>   than our body needs,
>   than our body can stand.

The fault, sometimes,
    lies with us.
We demand
    the instant pill
    to remove all aches and pains.
For a passing good,
    we risk lasting harm.

Our body
    is a magnificent instrument.
Within it
    are marvelous healing powers.
We have to stop
    interfering with those powers
    and treat our body
        with deep respect.

If we listen
    to our body
    carefully
        we can help heal ourselves.

6 – POTENTIAL

IF WE LISTEN
    to the kind of person
    we want to
        and can become,
            we can help heal ourselves.

We all have
    potential.
If we lived up
    to our potential,
        we could be a genius.
We have to acknowledge
    our potential
    and strive
        to fulfill it.

It is so easy
    to give in to
    negative
        feelings,
        thoughts,
        inhibitions.

In life,
    like a seaworthy ship,
    we must
        weigh anchor,
        face the buffeting of
        wind and wave,
        risk floundering,
        man the rudder
            to deliver the cargo.

It is the risk of failure
    that spurs us
    to greater effort;
        much like raising the marker
        after each high jump attempt.

To become the kind of person
    we want to and
    can become,
        we have to deal with
            bad memories,
            old hurts,
            disappointments.
These are
    convenient scapegoats.
To give in to them
    is self-defeating.

If we can blame
    someone else,
        we excuse
        our own lack of effort.

What others
    have done to us
        shame on them.

If we continue
    to use this
    as an excuse
        for not living our own lives,
            shame on us.

Our life
    is our responsibility!

If we are
    to reach our potential
        we have to recognize
        the devastating influence
            of a poor self-image.

If we view ourselves
    as failures,
        we will fail.
If we limit
    our expectations of ourselves,
        we cheat ourselves
            of richness,
            of growth.
We have to shed
    our self-imposed limits.

If we let them dominate
>   our lives,
>   we surrender to a tyrant.
This tyrant
>   is of our own making.
We created the monster
>   we have to destroy it.

Our attitude of mind
>   and disposition of heart
>   have a great influence
>   on our potential.

Fear of failure
>   is one of the biggest obstacles
>   to our growth,
>   to our development.

This fear may be so great,
>   we are so intent
>   on shielding our dignity,
>   on protecting our good name,
>   on playing it safe,
>   we do nothing.

We fear the risk
>   of exposing ourselves,
>   of possible disgrace,
>   of potential failure.
The result is
>   we remain in harbor.

A ship is not made for a calm harbor
>   and neither are we.

We have to seek
    and discover
        our talents,
        our gifts,
        our strength,
        our potential.
Let's look for
    the obvious gifts
        and the less obvious,
            those below the surface.

If we accept the challenge
    to change,
    to develop,
    to grow,
        we will become the person
        we want to and can become.

This is healing.

7 – HABITS

HABITS ARE OUR SECOND NATURE,
    even stronger than nature.

All of us
    are creatures of habit.
Habits
    influence our healing
        by promoting it,
        by impeding it.

Because of habits
    life runs smoothly.
If we had
    to relearn every action,
    as we did the first time,
        life would come to a stand still.

Habits are insidious.
They are
    deep seated
    well entrenched
        before we notice them.
But we are not born
    with them.
We acquire them
    step by step.

**Drinking Habits Need Special Attention.
You can easily test yourself in secret.**

1) Have you felt life would be better if you stopped drinking?
2) When you decide to stop, does the decision vanish almost overnight?
3) Do you switch to different kinds of drink hoping to stay sober?
4) Have you taken a drink in the morning this past year?
5) Do you envy those who can drink and not get drunk?
6) Have you had a drink-related problem in the past year?
7) Does your drinking cause problems for those you love?
8) Have you "conned" extra drinks at a party for fear you won't get enough?
9) Do you tell yourself you can stop any time you choose and still get drunk?
10) Have you missed days at work?
11) Do you have "blackouts"?
12) Do you wish people would mind their own business about your drinking?

If you **honestly** answered "yes" to four or more of these questions, you have a problem.

Just as a persistent drop of water
> creates a groove
> in the hardest granite,
>> so repeated action
>> carves a groove
>>> in our pattern of living.

Given a certain situation,
> a spontaneous,
> identical
>> response occurs.

Some habits
> arise
>> from ethnic, cultural background,
>> from occupation, environment,
>> from indolence, lassitude.

No matter how they arise,
> we do well
>> to listen to our habits —
>>> eating habits,
>>> sleeping habits,
>>> driving habits,
>>> working habits,
>>> drinking habits.

All have to be confronted
> to discover if they
>> hinder or
>> promote
>>> our healing.

Once we have determined
> how our habits affect us
>> good,
>> bad,
>>> we have to take
>>> decisive action.

Foster the good.

Eliminate the bad.

We may have to do violence
> and throw them
>> out the window.

We may have to coax them
> down the steps and
> out the door.

If we listen
> to our habits
> and act on what we hear,
>> we can heal ourselves.

8 – NATURE

LISTENING TO THE SOUNDS
    of nature
        can calm our nerves,
        settle our emotions.
When our nerves and emotions
    are under control,
    we are well on our way
        to healing ourselves.

Spend a week
    away from the city noise
        near a body of water,
        a lake or river's edge.

The sounds of the night
    create
        a symphony —
        soprano of the cicadae,
        alto of green frogs,
        bass of bull frogs
            for harmony —
            the hoot of the owls,
            the coo of the doves.

Listen
> to the gurgle of the brook
> rushing over the pebbles
>> as it fades into a lullaby
>> of the lazy river
>>> in the valley.

In the open spaces
> discover the aroma
>> of summer flowers,
>> of freshly mowed clover.

Scent
> the fog and fern
>> of autumn.

Experience
> the invigorating air of winter,
> the budding foliage of spring.

For peace of soul
> feast your eyes
>> on the multitude of flowers
>>> whose colors
>>> rival the rainbow.

For calm
> bask in the glory
>> of the sunlight.

Thrill to
> the crimson glow
>> of a sunset.

Watch
>   the gentle dawning
>   of a new day
>>   as the gold of heaven
>>>   tints
>>>   the linings
>>>>   of slowly drifting clouds.

This is the ointment
>   that heals the soul
>>   and spirit.

Note the refreshing effect
>   on the entire body
>>   as you run through the meadow
>>   and hear the wind
>>   whistle
>>>   through your hair.

Attend to the
>   soft spring shower
>>   that soothes the mind.

Savor the pure joy
>   of the silken spray
>   of the waterfall
>>   over the precipice.

Listen
>   to the rapturous drumbeat
>   of the raindrops
>   tattooing a melody
>>   on the tin roof.

Taste a snowflake.
Let one
    quietly
    drop in your palm
        and admire
        the exquisite symmetry.

For a therapeutic experience
    sleep under the sky
        and touch the stars
        that hang on invisible chains.
See how the world
    expands
        into infinity.

Observe
    the moon
    filter through the trees
    and like a ballet dancer
        flit
        across the forest floor.

Behold
    the irridescent ripple
    of the tiny cascade
        as the moonlight
        kisses
            the river's edge.

Everywhere in nature
    there is an abundance
    of little joys
        to heal body and soul.

This beauty
>   is God's signature
All creation
>   has
>   >   captured a beam,
>   >   imprisoned a spark
>   >   >   of the beauty of God.

God spoke
>   and all creation
>   became a glorious monstrance
>   >   to enshrine
>   >   the heart of its king.

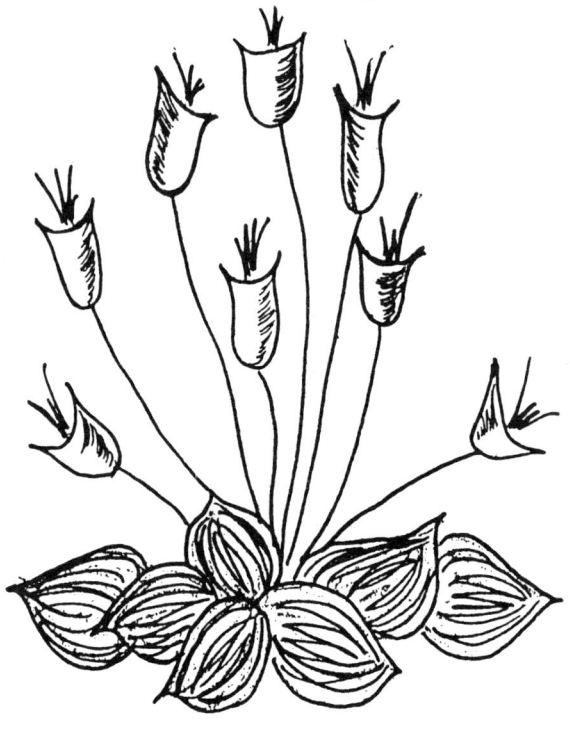

9-FORGIVENESS

LISTEN TO THE FORGIVENESS
    extended to us
        and we will
        help heal ourselves.

Because we belong
    to a wounded, marred nature
    we are easily victimized
        by natural instincts,
        by emotional tendencies,
        by acquired habits.
Often these go
    contrary
        to our sense of right and wrong.
We violate God's honor;
    we betray friends;
    we are unfaithful
        to our better selves.
We know we are
    weak,
    wounded,
    warped.

When we realize
> we have succumbed
> to unwholesome urges,
>> we are remorseful.

We are ashamed,
> confused,
> feel cheap and dirty.

It is healing to know:
> "Though your sins are like scarlet,
>> they may become white as snow.
> Though they be crimson red,
>> they may become white as wool."

Christ stressed that
> his father
>> was a forgiving father.

His parables
> bore the same message —
>> the prodigal son,
>> the Good Shepherd,
>> the lost sheep,
>> the lost coin.

His actions
> told the same story.

See how he treated
> Mary Magdalen,
> the woman taken in adultery,
> the woman at Jacob's well,
> the doubting Thomas,
> the betraying Peter.

His words
> have the same meaning —
>> "Have courage,
>>> your sins are forgiven you."
>> "Neither do I condemn you."
>> "Go and sin no more."

The forgiveness is there;
> we have to accept it.
If we accept it,
> we can be healed.

We need to accept
> the forgiveness
>> offered by others.
To know others
> are big enough to forgive
>> our meanness,
>> our stupidity
>>> is humbling and healing.

If our actions
> have shattered
>> a meaningful relationship,
>> it is refreshing to learn,
>> by the forgiveness of another
>>> the relationship can be restored.

It is important
> to accept
>> forgiveness from God,
>> forgiveness from others.

It is more important
> to accept forgiveness
>> from ourselves.

This may be difficult
> because
>> we see ourselves
>>> bereft of goodness,
>>> breaking resolutions,
>>> failing to improve.

It may be easier
> to forgive ourselves
> if we accept the fact
>> that human nature
>> is not perfect.

To be a perfectionist,
> to condemn oneself
>> for failure to achieve perfection,
>> is to forget
>>> our mortality.

Forgiveness of self
> may come easier
> if we distinguish
>> between spontaneous tendencies
>>> and deliberate decisions;
>> between involuntary imperfections
>>> and voluntary sins.

If God forgives,
> and he does;
> if man forgives
> and he does,
>> we all do well
>> to forgive ourselves.

10 – JOY

LISTEN TO THE JOY
   in life.
Joy has
   a healing value.

Many are ill
   in mind and body
   because
      they go through life
      like an accident
         looking for a place to happen.

The world teems
   with countless
   little joys.
All we have to do
   is open
      our eyes and ears.

We do not deny
   evil and sin
      bedevil us.
But this is no reason
   for glumness.

A good composer
> can take a false note,
> use it as a starting point
> > and create a new symphony.

God, like a good composer,
> starts with the false note
> > of evil and sin
> > > and creates the new symphony
> > > > of peace,
> > > > of reconciliation,
> > > > of forgiveness,
> > > > of redemption,
> > > > of love.

If we had not sinned,
> we could never
> > call God — Savior.

Some bemoan the fact
> we are living
> > in a vale of tears.

Granted,
> but this can be
> > a challenge.

Savonarola said:
> "No enemy, no fight.
> No fight, no victory.
> No victory, no crown."

Suffering
> is a universal experience.

It is the flotsam and jetsam
> of life.

But driftwood
> cast off by the sea
>> makes a beautiful mantelpiece.

It depends on
> one's perspective.

Stained glass windows
> from the outside
>> make little sense.

Inside the cathedral,
> you behold the masterpiece.

What makes the difference?
The perspective.

Perspective
> makes the difference
>> with suffering.

In itself
> suffering is a waste.

It is like
> an unsigned check —
>> valueless.

If we united our suffering
> with the redeeming suffering
>> of Christ,
>>> it takes on redeeming value.

The pity is,
> there is too much wasted suffering.

Perspective
> can give it value.

Some try to justify moroseness
    by claiming
        Christ did not smile.
If he did not smile,
    why should I?

I maintain
    Christ did smile.
An unsmiling Christ
    could never
        attract children.
And we know
    children mobbed him.

It was a smiling Christ
    who discovered
    Zacheus
    precariously perched
        in the sycamore tree.

In the home of Jairus
    after restoring the girl's health
    it was a smiling Christ
    who said:
        "Now give her something to eat."

Some complain:
    how can I be joyful
    when I am the victim of abuse?
Good trees with good fruit
    get sticks
        thrown after them.

You do not find
    sticks under trees
    with rotten apples.
If someone
    is throwing sticks at you,
        there may be something good
        in you.
If there was no good in you
    who would even bother?

Joylessness results
    if we follow
        the spirit of our times.
That spirit is a liar.
It promises joy
    in the morass
        of hedonism,
        of gluttony,
        of alcoholism,
        of drug abuse,
        of sex aberration.

If we
    elevate our sights,
    adjust our values,
    improve our goals,
        we will find joy.

That is healing.

11 – Compliments

IF WE LISTEN
> to the good things
> others say about us
>> we can help
>> heal ourselves.

When compliments
> come our way
> we can delight
>> in the positive evaluation
>> others put on our conduct.

Unfortunately,
> some have difficulty
>> handling compliments.

They are embarrassed,
> uncomfortable
> because
>> attention is on them.

They are front and center,
> in the spotlight.

Their sense of modesty
> loathes
>> showing off.

Others go
to the other extreme.
They look on a compliment
    as their lawful due.
They govern their lives
    by that word of approval.
They need compliments
    in order to function.
Often they put words
    in other people's mouths
        to force a compliment.
The way they formulate a question
    makes others compliment them.

Neither extreme
    is good.
A wholesome attitude
    lies between
        these extremes.

It is short-sighted
    to reject
        a compliment given in good faith.
A sincere compliment
    can be therapeutic.
It is a gift.
In it
    we see the goodness
        of the giver.

A COMPLIMENT REVEALS THE GOODNESS OF THE GIVER

Compliments given
    without ulterior motives
        are an expression
            of the respect
                someone has for us.
We all need
    this kind of affirmation.
If we accept it
    with gratitude
    as a generous gift,
        the attention
        remains on the giver
            and not on us.

A compliment gives
    a perspective of ourselves
    as seen
        through the eyes of others.
This is good to know.

Sometimes,
    we are so close to ourselves,
    so set against ourselves,
        that we don't see
        our own goodness.
A good, healthy
    self-appraisal
        must include our goodness.

A sincere compliment
    keeps us in touch
        with reality.
This is necessary
    for healing.

When we receive a compliment,
    we have an occasion
    to refer
        the goodness in us
        back to the primary source
                GOD.

If we listen
    with discretion,
    with discernment
        to compliments,
        we have a great source
           of healing.

12 – HUMOR

LISTEN TO HUMOR IN LIFE
    and we can heal ourselves.
It is so easy
    to be weighted down
    with the seriousness of life
        that we don't take time
        to smell the flowers.

A humorless life
    has a negative effect
    on our whole body
    and soul.
Humor
    is a part of humanity.
Of all God's creatures
    only man can laugh,
    at himself,
    at his world.
Nothing can be
    healthier.

A good rollicking laugh
    will rid us
    of the stuffy feeling
        that comes when
        we are so full of ourselves.

It is wholesome
 to recognize,
 to accept
  the paradoxes,
  the absurdities
   of life.
It is healthy
 to tolerate
 the frictions
  that arise from opposites.
To enjoy
 the frivolities of life
 is therapeutic.
We are told
 it is impossible
 physically,
 mechanically,
 chemically,
  to develop an ulcer
  if you know how to laugh,
   especially at yourself.

Without humor
 life is
  lugubrious and unbearable.

If, from time to time,
 we back away
 from the serious side of life,
  we see life has many meanings,
   some of them contradictory,
   some of them ambiguous.
And that is all right!

It is good
> to relax,
>> to allow ourselves
>>> to be caught off guard
>>>> without falling apart.
This experience
> refreshes and rejuvenates.

With a sense of the ridiculous
> we can laugh at ourselves;
> we can identify with humanity,
> we can understand that
> what happens to us
>> happens to others
>>> as well.
This kinship
> makes us more comfortable
>> with ourselves,
>> with others.
We accept ourselves
> without the frustration
>> of wanting to be
>>> someone else.
We accept others
> without putting them in a straitjacket
> and demanding change.
We allow them
> to be.

Humor
> makes us ready to accept
>> contradictions,
>> eccentricities,
>> foibles,
>> failures —
>>> our own and others.

If we listen to the lighter side of life,
> we can appreciate
>> the outrageous gaps,
>> the unexpected turn of events,
>> the tilting with windmills.

And laugh!

Laughter
> is a gift from God
> that enhances our life.

And we can make
> a worthy contribution to mankind
>> by bringing humor
>> into the lives of others.

Laughter
> is potent medicine.

Norman Cousins,
> painfully ill,
> locked himself in a motel
> with Marx Brothers movies.

Healthy laughter, he maintained,
> fortified his body against pain.

It gave him
> hours of pain-free, pill-free rest.

Ten minutes
> of solid belly laughs
> each day
>> will bring an abundance of health.

Humor
> reduces health-sapping tensions,
> relaxes tissues,
> exercises our organs,
> stimulates our heart,
> improves circulation.

It is a tranquilizer
> without side effects,
>> a miracle tonic
>> without the cost.

Humor
> maintains self-mastery,
> dispels anxiety and suspicion,
> provides excellent
>> coping mechanism.

Tickle
> your funny bone
>> every day.

Keep a file of
> laughter provoking events
> and use them,
>> daily,
>>> like vitamins.

Humor
> is healing.

13 – MUSIC

WE ARE SATURATED
    with music.
Music is within us,
    around us.
To listen to that music
    is healing.

Music, of the right kind,
    is relaxing,
    induces
        a meditative mood.
Music touches
    the center of our being.
It brings us back in tune
    with the beauty of living.

Music is
    as soothing as a luxury bath.
It is heavenly
    to be inundated
        by mellow tones,
        by easy rhythm,
        by enchanting harmony.

Our entire being
    resonates
        to joyous sounds.

It could be
    a lullaby,
        associated with
            tender care,
            loving embrace.

It could be
    that special melody
        that conjures up
        a delightful experience
            with someone we love.
"Our song."

Music has always been
    a part of human history.
In biblical times
    and now,
    music can raise
        mind and heart to God.
He is the source
    of all healing.

Music can
    affect moods,
    influence appetite,
    soothe the soul,
    calm anxieties,
    conquer fears,
    appease impulse to cruelty.

Music can affect
    pulse rate,
    heartbeat.
Respiration
    easily adapts to
        rhythm of music.
How often have we heard:
    "I could have danced
        all night."

Music can
    give rise to feelings
        of joy,
        of satisfaction,
        of tenderness,
        of love.
All of these
    help us feel good
        about ourselves.
When we feel good
    about ourselves,
        we release much
        of the healing power in us.

There is music
    to shop by.
Music to eat by,
    music to dance by,
        music to get well by.

To listen
    to music
        is to heal.

Listen to what I mean, not what I say

PART II

ACTIVE LISTENING,
Creative listening,
Redemptive listening,
Healing listening
    have this common element:
        listen to the meaning, not the word
        listen to the message, not the code.

To listen, in order to heal,
    is an art.
It takes effort.
It is threatening.

If I truly listen,
    I make myself vulnerable,
    risk my point of view,
    challenge my self-image,
    gamble on losing my secure position.

Too often
    I cling to my position
    and hear only
        what vindicates that position.

Too often
>   I tell you
>   what you mean
>>   instead of allowing you
>>   to tell me
>>>   what you mean.

Too often I try
>   to put my thoughts in your head
>   and my words in your mouth.

I often
>   get in the way
>   of my own listening.

I truly listen
>   if I can repeat,
>>   to your satisfaction,
>>   what you said,

I truly listen
>   when you agree
>>   I understand.

I have to listen
>   with my heart
>>   so it can vibrate with yours.

I have to listen
>   with my eyes
>>   so you can see I understand.

I have to listen
>   with my touch
>>   so you can feel one with me.

I have to listen
>   with my body
>>   so we can experience union.

14 – Teenagers

TEENAGERS NEED
    someone to listen
    to them.
Many of them
    are hurting
        and need healing.
We can help heal
    by listening.

We have to listen
    as they struggle
        to understand themselves,
        to test their strength,
        to achieve their independence.

We have to tune our ears
    to hear
        their fears about the future,
        their moments of self-doubt,
        the relentless power of
            peer pressure,
            the need to belong.

We have to listen
> as they strive to come to terms
>> with the merciless drive
>>> of their sexuality.

As they probe,
> experiment,
> discover,
>> try to understand
>> their need
>>> to strike out on their own.

This may be a serious threat
> because the values
> they may adopt
>> may not be the same as ours.

We must respect
> their freedom to choose.

Eventually,
> each of us
> must assume
> personal responsibility
>> for our own lives.

Listen
> when teenagers are afraid
> to trust us
>> because
>>> they dread misunderstanding;
>>> they dread rejection.

Trust needs
> time to develop.

We have to earn
> trust.

Like all of us,
    teenagers believe,
    if we reject
        their ideas,
        their values,
            we reject them.

This fact of life
    may be the cause of
        conflict,
        confrontation,
        dissension.

Tolerance, understanding
    are needed
    in great abundance.

We have to listen
    to teenagers
    as they build their own relationships
        which may exclude us.
If we listen,
    with patience,
    with understanding
        the exclusion
        may be only temporary.
If we force ourselves upon them,
    intrude into their privacy,
        we may never be allowed
        to enter.

If we listen,
> we will hear the many stages
> teenagers pass through —
>> "nobody cares,"
>> "nobody understands,"
>> "nobody listens,"
>> "I'm bored, nothing to do,"
>> "what is love?"
>> "what does the future hold?"
>> "I'm scared."

These are the down moments
> when it is especially necessary
> to listen to teenagers.

If we listen,
> we learn
>> they are experiencing
>>> a crisis of growth.

If we listen
> patiently,
> without judging,
> without condemning
>> but with love,
>>> the crisis
>>> will pass.

There are upbeat moments like —
> "I'm finding myself,"
> "I've found a cause,"
> "watch my sparks,"
> "get on my bandwagon."

These too
> we have to hear.

Listen, rejoice with them,
    as they find their world
        of friendships,
        of commitment,
        of belonging,
        of love.

We have to listen
    carefully
        because words do not always
        deliver the message.
Words often
    interfere with the message.
Listen to what
    teenagers mean
        not just what they say.
Try to grasp
    the message behind the words.
Try to
    decipher the code.

When we truly
    listen to teenagers,
    things begin to happen.

Masks crumble.
Bridges are built.
Channels are opened.
Hope rises.
Trust grows.
Confidence returns.
Meaning is clarified.
Relationships thrive.

Then when we say
> "I love you"
>> and it is important that
>> we do say it,
>>> there is a better chance
>>> we will be believed,
>>> our love accepted,
>>> our love returned.

To listen
> is to heal.

15 — DIVORCED

THE WOUNDS OF THE DIVORCED,
    if we listen,
        can be healed.
Listen as they ask:
    "who is to blame?"
Listen in their
    moments of anxiety.
Listen as they run
    from person to person
        seeking, desperately, for answers.
The search
    is relentless.

Their sense
    of personal worth
        is severely
        diminished.

They seriously doubt
    anyone understands.
Listen, anyway.

Listen
> as they refuse
> > to accept the facts.
They want to believe
> it is all
> > a bad dream.
In the morning
> it will be gone.

Listen
> as they stare out the window
> > hoping to see "that" one,
> as they wait at the phone
> > hoping for "that" call.

Listen
> as they misjudge,
> > refusing new opportunities,
> as they rant against
> > the opposite sex,
> > the phoniness of love,
> > the tyranny of the sex drive.

What they need
> more than anything
> > is someone just to listen.
The feelings of aloneness
> are unbearable.
With loneliness
> comes the fearful realization
> > of overwhelming responsibility,
> > of consuming fear,
> > of deep depression.

The depression is awful,
    no dates,
    questionable loyalties,
    futile attempts to
        get at the bottom of it all.

Listen
    as jealousy rears its head
        when they see former partner
        survive, thrive,
            get back into life's stream,
            happy, and seemingly unscathed.

Listen
    as they question new involvements
        (their own and their former
        partner's)
    as they make comparisons
        between what they now have,
        and what they had.
They need
    affirmation and reassurance.

Listen
    as they deal
        with the world's attitude
            toward the divorced.
It can be brutal
    and unkind.

Listen
    as they try to sort out
        likes,
        wants,
        longings,
        desires.
They need this clarification
    in order to cope.

Listen
    as they slowly and painfully
        accept reality,
    as they begin to see
        opportunities
            of growth,
            of finding self,
            of adapting to a new life-style,
            of opening to others,
            of building trust again,
            of falling in love.

If we listen,
    life can gradually
    take on
        a tolerable normalcy.

They can heal.
They can live.

MAY THE LORD BLESS YOU

Blessed are they who understand
my faltering step and palsied hand.

Blessed are they who know that my ears today
must strain to catch the things they say.

Blessed are they who seem to know
that my eyes are dim and my wits are slow.

Blessed are they who looked away
when coffee spilled on the table today.

Blessed are they with a cheery smile
who stop to chat for a little while.

Blessed are they who never say:
"You've told that story twice today."

Blessed are they who know the way
to bring back memories of yesterday.

Blessed are they who make it known
that I'm loved, respected, not alone.

Blessed are they who know my loss
to find the strength to carry the cross.

Blessed are they who ease the days
of my journey home in loving ways.

16 — ELDERLY

MUCH OF OUR ATTITUDE
    is geared
        toward youth.
As people live longer,
    new problems arise.

It is a misconception
    to categorize older people
        as sweet, loving, kind
        or as crabby, crotchety, difficult.
What they were
    when young,
        they remain in later years.
A young autocrat
    does not become docile.
A vain, frivolous youth
    does not become
        a self-effacing adult.

People,
    young and old
    are to be treated
        as individuals.

It is unjust
>   to lump them together
>   in one class.

It is not true
>   that the elderly
>   want a safe and cozy nest,
>   regardless of cost.

Much unhappiness comes
>   from others who are always
>   "doing what is for your best."

This also
>   generates
>   anger and resentment.

They resent hearing:
>   "act your age."

Who is to say
>   how the elder
>   should act?

Let's not
>   underestimate their ability.

They are
>   remarkably tough.

It is wrong
>   to ignore their capabilities,
>   to undermine their initiative.

Who are we to say
>   they cannot
>   change careers —
>   no matter what age!

Listen to them.

plan **with** elderly people, not **for** them

It is better
>   and more acceptable
>   to plan with them
>   instead of for them.

To be of help
>   we have to listen
>   to the pain of being uprooted,
>   to the dread of change,
>   to the fear of loss of freedom.

Listen as they struggle
>   for independence,
>   for self-respect.

Listen to the exasperation
>   as they struggle
>   to do for themselves
>   and still need help
>   even to do for themselves.

Listen
>   as they alienate,
>   without knowing it,
>   the people who love and care.

Don't turn a deaf ear
>   when they are angry because
>   of limited mobility,
>   of prolonged suffering,
>   of need for more rest,
>   of lack of energy.

Listen
>	as they wonder aloud
>	what is in store for them
>>	because they no longer contribute.

They question
>	their usefulness,
>	their worth.

They cling to their possessions
>	because they are so vulnerable,
>>	easily confused,
>>	easily taken advantage of.

Listen
>	and respond
>>	as they crave
>>>	physical touch,
>>>	body embrace.

The life of the elderly
>	can be
>>	so lonely.

They need to know
>	that they are
>>	loved,
>>	cherished,
>>	accepted.

They need
>	affirmation!

Listen
>	as they tell you about
>	interminable waiting.

It is true.

Nobody has to wait
>so often,
>so long,
>>as the elderly.

Listen
>as they recall memories.

So what
>if you heard the stories before?

So what
>if they live in the past?

The past
>for many of the elderly
>>is all they have.

Let them share it
>as we listen.

We can help the elderly
>more than we realize
>>if we
>>>just listen.

17 – BEREAVED

WE CAN HEAL
    the hurt and the loss
    of the bereaved
        if we listen.

It is important
    not to short-circuit
    the grief
        by inane cliches.

A free and accepted
    expression of grief
        is necessary
            to work through it.

We do well
    to listen
    as the bereaved
    talk about their anguish.

Don't clutter the conversation
    with trivia
        to avoid the subject.
Let them talk!

They need someone
    to share
        their present sorrow,
        their joys of the past,
        their good memories and bad,
        their yearning for a return
            of the love and contact
            they once had.
They need someone
    to listen
        as they talk about the deceased.

They need someone
    to listen
    as they talk
        on their own terms,
        in their way,
        at their pace,
        in their time.
Let's be patient.
Don't pressure them.

If your presence
    prompts them to talk,
        listen.

If your presence
    does not prompt them to talk
        just being there,
            in silence,
                is enough.
Your presence
    speaks volumes.

If tears come,
    don't panic.
Tears
    are therapy.
Tears can cleanse
    sorrow,
    anger,
    regrets,
    guilt,
    remorse.
Let the tears flow.

Listen without judging
    as they express
        anger at God,
        resentment about being alone,
        fears about the future,
        self-pity over personal loss,
        regret over lost opportunities,
        feelings of guilt.

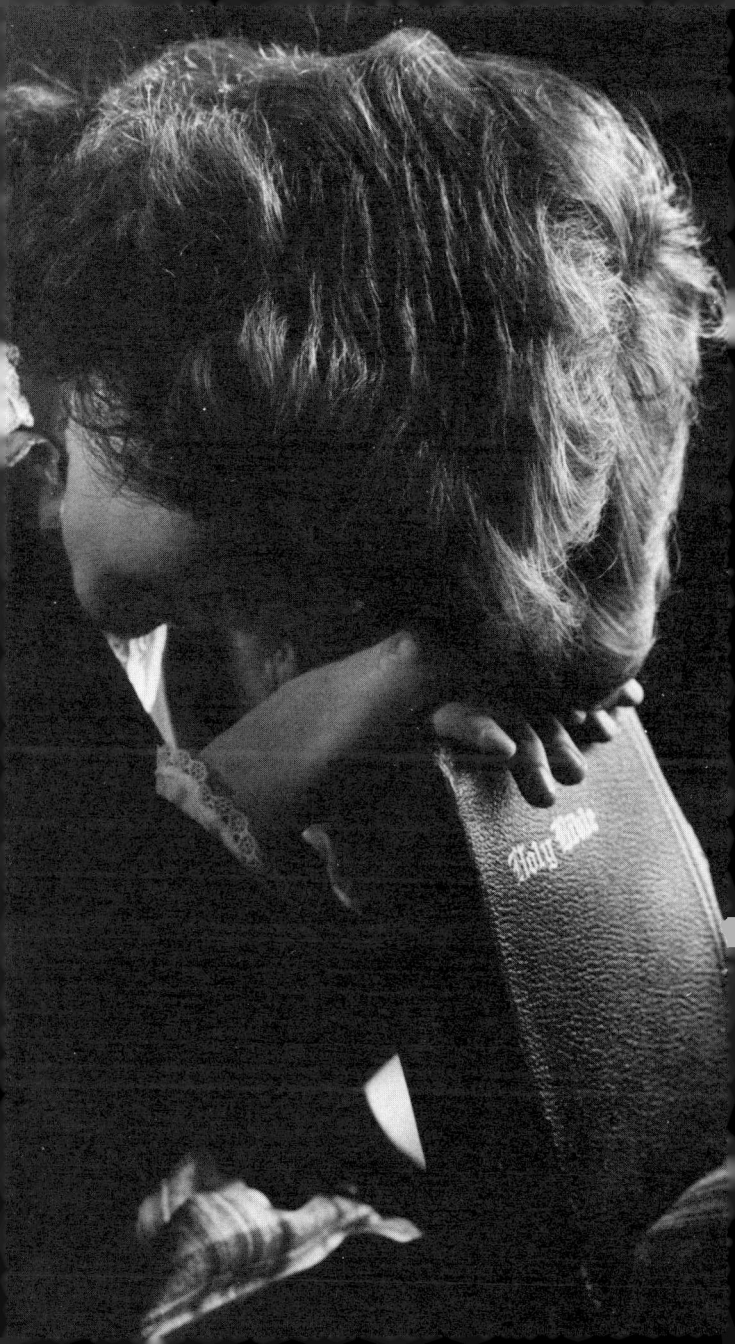

Let them tell you
> about
>> difficulty in concentration,
>> preoccupation with death,
>> feeling a presence,
>> hearing voices,
>> dreaming strange dreams,
>> loathing to go out,
>> yearning to stay home, alone,
>> strong desire to drop out.

To aid the bereaved
> listen.

Above all it is necessary
> to listen after the funeral
>> when sympathy cards are read,
>> when acknowledgments are written,
>> when routine sets in.

The loss is more acute
> in the lonely hours
> when no one is around,
>> no one comes to listen,
>> no one comes to share.

This is when the bereaved
> need someone to listen
>> patiently
>>> until they accept reality,
>>> attempt new ventures,
>>> affirm love,
>>> resume living.

OUR BELOVED LIVE ON IN FOND MEMORIES

When grief
    is defused,
        life can resume.
Life will not be the same.
That is impossible.
Hopefully
    it will be good,
        even better.

Death may deprive us
    of physical contact,
    of tactile presence,
    of loving embrace.

Still
    loved ones live on
        in fond memories,
        pleasant recall,
        happy recollection.

Loved ones live on
    in the seeds they planted,
    the deeds they have performed,
    the influence they exerted,
    the lives they lived
        in the circles
        in which they moved.

Life is not ended.

Life is merely
    changed.

Life will go on!

AFTER WORD

May I always be aware of the wonder of people. They come in all sizes, shapes and colors. They are young and old, important and lowly, quick and slow, intelligent and unlettered, neighbors and strangers, friends and enemies.

Unfortunately, each of us seems to be going our own way with private passion and aspiration locked in the tiny world of self. We may try to communicate, to share, to give; but the limited horizon of our personal concerns impedes the effort.

I want to be tuned in to the worlds spinning behind those faces. I am sure they are fascinating worlds, teeming with memories, experiences, philosophies, ambitions, dreams, anxieties, worries, hurts, and hates.

I want to listen, truly listen, when these people speak in overt or subtle ways. They are opening the small doors of their worlds and trying to let me enter. I have to be mindful it is a risk for them, for me. I may never be able to enter completely but I can give so much and receive so much — if I listen.

I have to learn not to barge off in my own conceits, waiting in half-deaf exasperation to say my piece, to tell my story. It is a privilege to be invited even to the doorsteps of these worlds.

I want to identify with these people, taste their tears as well as my own, love and be loved, accept and be accepted, rejoice and share joy.

They live and feel, breathe and think the same as I do. The more I become aware of the wonder of people, the more I become aware of the wonder of myself.

Photo Credits:
Ed Carlin 88, 112; Mary K. Cichowski 44, 56; Hope Cook 10; Rohr Engh 21; Vivienne della Grotta 16, 25, 30, 41, 49, 59, 75, 96; David S. Strickler (Strix Pix) 34, 90; Robert Taylor 63, 69, 117.

**For the cassette

RELAX. You can do it!

send $10.00 to author
5045 S. Laflin Street
Chicago, IL 60609

PUBLICATIONS of
Albert J. Nimeth O.F.M.

Books:

THERE IS MORE TO LIFE**
I LIKE YOU just BECAUSE*
of course, I LOVE YOU*
tenderly I CARE*
To LISTEN is to HEAL*
INSTANT INSPIRATION**
SUDDEN THOUGHTS***

Pamphlets:

Novice Instruction Outlines**
Getting Wise in Ways of God**
To Live the Gospel**
Guidelines of St. Francis**
The Spirit We Need**
Popular Life of St. Francis**
In Time of Your Sorrow**
Life is Beautiful**
Words to Get Well By*
Joy — Nature's Best Remedy*

---

*Available
**Unavailable
***Available from *Daughters of St. Paul.*
                                      New title

"LEARNING CHRIST"

Teach me, my Lord, to be sweet and gentle in all the events of life — in the thoughtlessness of others, in the insincerity of those I trusted, in the unfaithfulness of those on whom I relied.

Let me put myself aside, to think of happiness of others, to hide my little pains and heartaches, so that I may be the only one to suffer from them.

Teach me to profit by the suffering that comes across my path.

Let me so use it that it may mellow me, not harden nor embitter me; that it may make me patient, not irritable, that it may make me broad in my forgiveness, not narrow, haughty and overbearing.

May no one be less good for having come within my influence. No one less pure, less true, less kind, less noble for having been a fellow-traveler in our journey toward ETERNAL LIFE.

As I go my rounds from one distraction to another, let me whisper from time to time, a word of love to You. May my life be lived in the supernatural, full of power for good, and strong in its purpose of sanctity.

Give us, Lord, a listening Heart